TEACHING YOUNG CHILDREN

A GUIDE FOR TEACHERS AND LEADERS

REVISED EDITION

MARYJANE PIERCE NORTON

DISCIPLESHIP RESOURCES

P.O. BOX 840 • NASHVILLE,TN 37202-0840

Scripture quotations are from the New Revised Standard Version of the Bible, copyright © 1989 by the Division of Christian Education of the National Council of the Churches of Christ in the USA. All rights reserved. Used by permission.

ISBN 0-88177-229-1

Library of Congress Catalog Card No. 97-66968

Revised Edition

DR229

CONTENTS

ALSO AVAILABLE FROM DISCIPLESHIP RESOURCES

TEACHING THE BIBLE TO ELEMENTARY CHILDREN
by Dick Murray (revised 1997)

Drawing on years of experience as a Christian educator both in the church and in academic settings, Dick Murray offers an insightful tour of the way of the Bible with children and the way of children with the Bible. Chapters discuss strategies required for teaching the Bible to younger elementary children as compared to those required for teaching the Bible to older elementary children, the art of storytelling, the role of memorization "for participation," and additional creative approaches for teaching the Bible to children. Two final chapters outline a program for training teachers and give suggestions for a congregation's presentation of Bibles to children.

HELPING CHILDREN FEEL AT HOME IN CHURCH
by Margie Morris (revised 1997)

With light humor and friendly conversation, Margie Morris gives clear advice and concrete suggestions about every family's spiritual needs, which begin in the home. Chapters deal with children in worship; helping children understand the order of worship; baptism and Communion; church music; visual arts in worship; children as worship leaders; congregational climate, including the pastor's role; and family climate. All chapters end with a suggested activity to explore faith matters in a way that engages the entire family. A chapter-by-chapter discussion guide is provided for adults who wish to study and discuss the book in a group setting.

YOUNG CHILDREN— WHO ARE THEY?

To teach well, you need to know children—who they are, what they are like, what they can and cannot do. Such learning begins on a general level as you seek to understand basic characteristics and needs of the age levels you teach. That understanding then becomes the basis for learning all that you can about each individual child in your class, which learning in turn adds to your general knowledge of children. This book gives basic information about teaching young children and will start you on the journey of learning all that you can about each special person in your class.

INFANTS

If you have volunteered to work with the youngest children in your church, you may not see yourself as a teacher, but you are. During their first years children change more rapidly than they will at any other time in their lives. It's important for you to know and recognize what babies are learning and what skills they are gaining. You can then plan ways of relating to them that promote growth and development.

Newborn Babies

Newborn babies can see, hear, feel, smell, and taste. They see faces and objects best when these are only eight to ten inches away from their eyes. A newborn can distinguish sounds and may show interest in the human voice. Newborns spend most of their time sleeping.

WHAT CAN YOU DO?

Establish eye contact with the newborn. Talk to and smile at the baby. Hold the baby close. Use red and yellow or black and white objects to help get the baby's attention. Make sure that the baby is comfortable; and above all, love the baby.

At Four Weeks

Most parents first bring their babies to the church nursery when the babies are four to six weeks old. Parents should be discouraged from bringing babies any younger because of the risk of exposure to germs.

At four weeks a baby is beginning to recognize her mother. The baby will often open and close her mouth when someone speaks and will quiet down at the sound of her mother's voice.

A four-week-old can follow a swinging toy in a ninety-degree range and will turn her head toward sound. The baby can hold her head up momentarily if in a sitting position and can lift her head up momentarily if lying down.

WHAT CAN YOU DO?

Keep hugging, talking, touching, and loving the baby. Show her bright colors. Play with toys where the baby can see you.

Sing to the baby, holding her close. The baby not only receives the gift of music but also enjoys feeling vibrations in your body.

All babies up to about four months of age need to suck. Check with parents to see if they let their baby have a pacifier; know where to locate it if the baby needs it.

At Eight Weeks

At this age a baby can definitely recognize his mother. He smiles when talked to. He can follow a swinging toy in a full side-to-side range. The baby's eyes follow moving people. When helped into a sitting position, he can keep his head up, although it bobs forward occasionally.

WHAT CAN YOU DO?

Smile back at the baby. Continue to display brightly colored objects. Talk to and sing to the baby. Introduce musical toys. Keep hugging and loving him.

At Sixteen Weeks

The baby now smiles regularly, holds up her head and turns toward sounds, swallows soft food, and grasps objects. She will sit and stare at people. She can play with a rattle. She may try to reach for objects but will often overshoot her mark.

A four-month-old has a perfect toy with her at all times; she is fascinated with her own hands. She'll watch them as they wave in the air, then bring them together. She may clasp them and then be unable to unclasp them.

WHAT CAN YOU DO?

Give four-month-old babies grasping toys. Introduce pat-a-cake. Let the baby grasp your finger.

Use crib mobiles with bright colors. Entertain the baby with unbreakable mirrors. Let the baby roll over on the floor. And, of course, continue to hug and love her.

At Twenty-four Weeks

By six months most babies have doubled their birth weight and their first tooth has appeared. The child will try to sit alone, will hold out his hands and indicate his desire to be lifted up, and can feed himself a cracker.

The baby recognizes himself in the mirror and delights in smiling and talking to himself in the mirror. Some babies may begin to show a fear of strangers at about this age.

WHAT CAN YOU DO?

Gently bounce the baby on your lap. Play peekaboo with the baby. Introduce toys with shapes. Hold the baby up on his feet so that he can practice standing. Play with unbreakable mirrors, smiling together at your images in the mirror. Continue using music and keep on hugging and loving.

At Thirty-six Weeks

The nine-month-old will respond to her own name and will imitate sounds. She will try to establish contact with another person by coughing or yelling or making some other noise to attract the person's attention.

The baby will often imitate the sound you make or will make her own noises by banging on a table, clicking her tongue, or knocking toys together.

The baby can now pick up small objects between her finger and thumb and will often try to put these objects into her mouth. By nine months, most babies are crawling or scooting.

WHAT CAN YOU DO?

Imitate the sounds the baby makes and encourage her to imitate you. Provide clean floor space for the baby to crawl on and explore. Let the baby hold on to your fingers and try to walk.

Babies by now have developed object permanence. Up until now if something left the baby's field of vision, it ceased to exist in her mind. If you hide a toy by covering it with a blanket, a young baby will not look for it. But when a child develops object permanence, she will try to pull away the covering to get to the hidden object. Object permanence is the beginning of abstract thought, which is the basis for imagination, fantasy play, and reading. The child now has a picture in her mind of things not in sight. Use books with thick pages or plastic books with the baby. Play variations of peekaboo. Let the baby gaze out of windows.

Talk constantly to the baby, telling her of your love and of God's love. Keep talking to, hugging, and loving the child.

At One Year

Many one-year-olds can say two or three words. They understand many more. These children can wave bye-bye and understand that either they are leaving or someone else is leaving. This understanding often leads to tears when parents leave their child in the church nursery.

One-year-olds engage in games. One favorite is to drop objects so that you will pick them up. Another is to repeat an activity again and again so that you will clap for them.

Many one-year-olds are walking alone or by holding on to one object and then another. They move purposefully around the room, exploring, tasting, testing anything in their path.

WHAT CAN YOU DO?

Read to the child. Use books with simple illustrations. Make up your own words instead of reading the book word for word. Show pictures and make noises, car sounds, and animal sounds, pairing the sound with the appropriate object.

Work on building the child's vocabulary. Talk about God and about things in God's world and have short prayers with the child: "Thank you, God, for sunshine and flowers" or "Thank you, God for yummy crackers to eat." Help the child walk. And keep hugging and loving the child.

✔ How Do You Nurture Faith in Infants?

All faith is based on trust. As a child learns that adults satisfy her needs, she begins to trust. Her trust in adults forms the basis for trusting God.

Your use of tapes or CD's, simple songs, and short prayers can help the child build words about God into his vocabulary. He begins to associate the love and concern shown by you, the teacher, with the love and concern of God.

Let the child play with mirrors; and as she laughs and talks to her own image, repeat again and again, "You are a child of God, and God loves you." These words encourage the child to make the connection between God and herself.

Use bright, colorful Bible storybooks with lots of big pictures and few words, as well as other books. Look for books that concentrate on the senses and on the world around us. Connect the pictures in the books with God by saying thanks to God for what is pictured and for our wonderful world.

YOUNG CHILDREN

Rapid change and growth continue through the preschool years. During these years, children gain control of their bodies, develop language skills, learn to relate to and play with other children, and grow in faith. The way to guide their growth differs somewhat at each age level. Teachers should use activities and techniques that best suit the needs of the child from the time the child is a toddler until he or she is ready to enter the world of the school-age child at six or seven years of age.

Toddlers (one- to two-year-olds)

Toddlers are so named because they toddle with a slow, uncertain gait, falling often. Once they master walking, however, they move to a run and stay in constant motion.

Toddlers fight against confinement: highchairs, car seats, playpens. They've found freedom in walking, and they are eager to investigate every inch of space.

Toddlers are unaware of danger; and having a short memory, they rarely associate past hurts with present action.

Toddlers are egocentric. They are concerned about the here and now and think that the world revolves around them. Toddlers have just begun to experience independence, and they try to exercise that independence in many ways. "Me do it" and "No" are two ways they assert themselves. As you work with toddlers, remember that *no* is not a rejection of you; it is a word of independent expression that can mean, "What are my choices?"

In the classroom, toddlers engage in solitary play. They see other children as objects and treat them as such. They poke another child's eyes, pull hair, or pat another child as a way of exploring the child as they would an object. Toddlers can be aggressive toward one another, not because they intend to hurt another person, but because they are assertive explorers. They need to keep learning acceptable ways to treat others.

Because toddlers have a short attention span, they move quickly from one activity to another. Both toddlers and the adults working with them become frustrated if they are forced to spend time as part of a large group in one activity.

At the same time, toddlers don't like change and appreciate routines. Your saying the same words to introduce and explain the same activity each day is important to them.

Although the toddler's control over his large muscles is increasing, he still has trouble with fine-muscle control. Activities that require use of the hands to accomplish a focused task can be frustrating and may result in temper tantrums.

WHAT CAN YOU DO?

Provide a classroom with space for toddlers to walk, bend, climb, and crawl. Make sure your space is clean, since many objects still end up in a toddler's mouth.

Have a routine for your class. Each Sunday follow a schedule with time for play, time for a story, time for a snack, and so forth. Plan for children to engage in activities by themselves or in small groups. Instead of trying to call toddlers together into a group, simply start an activity and let them join in one by one. Work with one child or a few children at a time.

Set limits in the classroom. You will need to guard the rights of each child, protecting the children from one another.

Sharing is difficult for toddlers. They aren't ready for this concept. Provide more than one of the children's favorite activities and toys. Having enough things for these children to explore and enjoy is more important and helpful than making them share a favorite toy under duress.

✔ How Do You Nurture Faith in Toddlers?

As the adult in the class, you are a model of kindness, empathy, sharing, and caring for toddlers. Continue to build trust in the children. Toddlers should be able to depend on seeing the same teachers week by week, meeting in the same classroom, hearing the same songs and stories, and enjoying the same activities again and again. This repetition reinforces trust—the feeling that I know what's waiting for me. I can depend on my teacher; and since my teacher speaks of God with love, God must be like my teacher; so I can trust in God.

Although toddlers are egocentric, they can express kindness and empathy. Seeing you express this care helps them show care to one another. They will, like you, give pats on the back, kiss a hurt knee, cry along with another.

You are also a role model for sharing. In this role pair your actions with words that explain what you are doing. "Today I brought cookies. I will share my cookies with each of you. When we share, we all enjoy cookies. Thank you, God, for cookies."

Toddlers grow in faith as they hear you pray, thanking God, and as they hear you talking about God's love. They are building their vocabulary and will pick up words and phrases from you, repeating these in snatches at home.

Music is a useful tool in helping toddlers build vocabulary. Teach toddlers simple songs about God's love. Pairing words with actions helps toddlers know the songs. They will learn the actions first and then some phrases and words to the songs.

Two-Year-Olds

Two-year-olds are continuing to perfect their physical skills. They have more control over their bodies, walking and moving better and beginning to use the small muscles in their hands.

Two-year-olds can jump, hop, roll, and climb well. They enjoy movement games and moving to music. As they improve their body control, they become ready for toilet training. Their changing toileting needs can produce both frustration and a sense of accomplishment for the two-year-olds in your class.

Being perceived as a terrible two is a side effect of the developing autonomy of the two-year-old. As he gains more control, he wants to exercise more control over his environment. But sometimes the only way he can assert himself is to yell a resounding "No!"

Another reason for the term *terrible twos* is that two-year-olds are stubborn; they are attached to "their" stuff and will often shout, "Mine!" (whether the object is theirs or not). This stubborn possessiveness causes two-year-olds to grab toys, scream, throw tantrums, and generally engage in aggressive behavior. All of these behavioral actions can and do happen in the two-year-old classroom. But all of these actions can also happen with toddlers and with three- to five-year-olds.

The two-year-old suffers a great deal of frustration because of language. She understands many more words than she can express. When words fail her, she bites, kicks, screams. She cannot verbalize her feelings, so she expresses them the only way she can—physically. As she learns to say more words and phrases, words will take the place of action. Most two-year-olds start the year with a vocabulary of about two hundred words and end the year with a vocabulary of about one thousand words.

Two-year-olds engage in parallel play with other children. Although they don't engage in interactive play, they do the same things side by side. They love being near other children, and they enjoy imitating one another. If one starts a noise or a word, others repeat the same word or noise.

Two's have a short attention span; and except for times when they are engaged in one-on-one activity with an adult, they move quickly through activities. They may return to activities they have done previously and do them again, or they may do something else that catches their attention. They are seldom bored.

WHAT CAN YOU DO?

Give children power in their room. Plan activities that offer them real choices: "We're going to paint today. Would you like to use red paint or blue paint?" "It's time for our story. Would you like to walk or to hop to the story circle?"

Asking, "Would you like to hear a story now?" is not a real choice if that's what you've planned for the children to do at that particular time. Such questions are open invitations for two-year-olds to assert their independence and their right to make choices. Be prepared for a resounding "No!" Better still, don't ask.

Give two-year-olds words to show emotions. "You are angry at Tyne because he took the red ball." "It's frustrating when the puzzle pieces won't go back into the puzzle." "It makes you sad when Mommy leaves to go to her Sunday school class." By giving two-year-olds words, you give them power over the scary feelings that they can express only through body actions.

As with the toddlers, do first and explain as you do. Sit down at the table and start pounding and pushing a lump of play dough. Talk as you do so, inviting the children to join you in making snakes or cookies or cups or smiley faces.

Plan ways to involve the children's senses. Instead of just telling a story, use puppets as you tell it. Instead of talking about a flower, bring a flower into the classroom for children to hold and sniff and enjoy.

Remember their short attention span and don't expect two-year-olds to sit together working on a group project or listening to a story for an extended time period. Allow lots of time for free play and work with a few children at a time.

As with toddlers, set limits in the classroom. You need have only two rules in your classroom: 1) You are not allowed to hurt other people. 2) You are not allowed to hurt toys or equipment in our room. Repeating these rules several times each Sunday will help children learn to care for one another and for their room.

✔ How Do You Nurture Faith in Two-Year-Olds?

You are the example. Show the children ways to live together as Jesus would want us to live. Demonstrate kindness, empathy, understanding, sharing, and forgiveness. Matching actions with words helps two-year-olds begin to understand what you do and why you do it.

Express your faith in an open manner. Talk about God's love, God's world, and Jesus as a friend to children. Pray with the children, keeping prayers short and addressing your prayers to God. Let the children volunteer things they want to thank God for.

Use music. Two-year-olds love to move to music. Don't worry that they cannot repeat the words to hymns and songs. Select and use the same songs again and again throughout the year. The children will gradually learn the words if they hear them often.

Tell stories of the faith. Keep a Bible in your room and show children where the story you are telling is in the Bible. Repeat stories often. Tell them with puppets, with teaching pictures or posters, with flannelboard, or with fingerplays. Act them out; put them to music. Make sure that the stories are short, lasting a maximum of five minutes at the most.

Three-Year-Olds

It's not unusual for a teacher of three-year-olds to smile broadly as he talks about his class. For the most part, three's are happy, cooperative children. They like to please and want to do what is right. They love to be praised and work hard to hear the praise of adults.

Three-year-olds are charmers. They smile to win you over, climb into your lap for hugs, and notice your feelings. Three-year-olds prefer adult attention on a one-on-one basis to having to share the adult in a group.

Three-year-olds are beginning to play cooperatively. They play and interact best with one or two children at a time. They are aware, however, of the larger group and will notice when a child is missing.

Children at this age are active, often on the run. They are curious, but only briefly, since their attention span is still short. They will move quickly from painting to playing with puppets, to building with blocks, to making cookies, to working a puzzle.

Even in the midst of newfound confidence, a three-year-old can still be unsure and frightened. A child who has entered class quite happily may suddenly start crying for Mommy or Daddy.

Three may be the year when fears appear. Suddenly the child is frightened of monsters, frightened by the dark, frightened of riding on escalators. One way three-year-olds deal with fear or loneliness is through imaginary friends. A three-year-old may bring her imaginary friend to Sunday school and may need an activity book, a chair, and a snack for the friend. Because being bad is also frightening, since it makes adults angry, this imaginary friend may be the culprit of bad behavior.

Three-year-olds have better control of the fine muscles in their hands. Using scissors becomes fascinating because three-year-olds can finally manage them. A child may enjoy snipping paper into scraps but still is not ready to cut carefully along printed lines. Coloring, painting, and playing with play dough all show the child's increased skill. The resulting creations may not look like real objects to others, but they are real to the child.

Having created something, however, the child may then show little interest in it. At this age the process, rather than the product, is the child's accomplishment.

Exploring the world is a favorite activity of three-year-olds. They notice many things about the natural world and ask, "What?" "Why?" "Where?" and "When?"

WHAT CAN YOU DO?

Be ready to praise your three-year-olds. Point out ways they have grown and what they can do now that they couldn't do when they were younger.

Listen to the children. Take their questions seriously. Give them short answers and the same courtesy you would give an adult.

Encourage children to be curious, and take advantage of teachable moments—times when you simply stop and answer a child's questions instead of hurrying to the next planned activity.

"Let me do it" is a favorite request of three-year-olds. Plan activities in which the children can actually do what is required. A craft completed by the teacher may look nice but does nothing to enhance that feeling of "I can do it."

Plan ways children can help care for the room and for one another. Instead of pouring juice for the children, let them pour it. The pouring will take longer and might be messier, but now is the time when you need to help children feel capable and good about what they can do. Do not fuss if the pouring results in spills. Acknowledge that you sometimes spill things too.

Plan plenty of time for free play and active games. Encourage children to take turns. Help with the beginning and end of each person's turn. Say, "Now it is time for Bonnie to splash in the water," as you guide Bonnie to the splashing pan and suggest another task or activity to occupy the attention of the current splasher. A timer with a bell can help time turns.

Imaginative play is important for three-year-olds. Standing at the play stove, they become a cook or a mommy or daddy or a grandparent, playing out the way they see the world.

✔ How Do You Nurture Faith in Three-Year-Olds?

You are the model for faith. Lead children in sharing, taking turns, helping someone who is hurt, saying please and thank you. As you express your faith, children will imitate your behavior.

Accepting children as they are and helping them feel good about what they can do helps them accept the statement "God loves you." Helping three-year-olds succeed underlines their belief that "I am good. I am a child of God."

Three-year-olds have a strong sense of "mine." Church for them is "*my* room" and "*my* teacher." The love they have for their room and their teacher spills over into the larger church.

Three-year-olds grow in faith as you share your faith. When you talk about God's love, when you tell them stories from the Bible, when you show love to others, you nurture their faith.

Because three-year olds now have many more words and can talk in sentences, they can say their own prayers as well as repeat ones you teach them. They are aware of God's gifts and are eager to say thanks to God for rainbows and butterflies and rocks.

The Bible is a special book for three-year-olds because it contains stories of Jesus. You help reinforce this feeling about the Bible when you show the children where the stories you tell are found.

Three-year-olds identify with Jesus as a baby because they have been told about themselves as babies. They also learn that Jesus was a man who loved children, and they return this love.

Four-Year-Olds

Suddenly the cuddly three-year-old becomes a noisy, messy, extremely active four-year-old. With boundless energy, she sets out to explore the world. Highly curious, she investigates everything, asking endless questions that often begin with *why*.

Many four-year-olds like to see how things work. If a toy in the four-year-old classroom is not well made, therefore, it might not last the year. An attempt to figure out how that train moves around that track may result in train pieces scattered around the room. Or a pop-up book may end up with all the pop-ups torn out as the result of a child's wanting to find out what makes them pop up. The child's goal is not to be destructive—it's to find out how things work.

This year is the one for developing special friends. Four-year-olds enjoy their friends. They also sometimes band together and ignore those who were friends just the day before.

The four-year-old, wanting to figure out everything, tries to come up with logical explanations. These often are based on his intuition, however, since fact and fantasy still are not separate in his mind. As a result, his explanations may sound like storytelling. In explaining how the plant was knocked off the shelf, a four-year-old may tell of a great monster from outer space who landed a spaceship right where the plant was and knocked it to the floor. This use of imagination in trying to say that the occurrence was an accident is illogical to adults but often perfectly logical to the child.

Because their imaginations are so vivid, four-year-olds delight in pretending and dramatic play. Family living activities become more elaborate. Instead of simply cooking hot dogs at the stove, four-year-olds shop for the groceries, cook, clean up, and take food to neighbors. In their pretending they imagine themselves as big and capable, confident and unafraid. Such fantasizing is important for their development.

A four-year-old rarely sits still. Even when her body is still, her hands or feet or tongue may still be going. But four-year-olds need to have relaxation and rest time built into their schedules. Their bodies need help in slowing down from unending activity.

Four-year-olds are experimenting with words. It isn't unusual to hear them trying out swearwords and bathroom words. They do so partly to test adult reaction and partly as an attempt at humor.

Four-year-olds find life fun and funny. They like silly humor and laugh wildly at one another. If one child slips off her chair and everyone laughs, others will slip off their chairs and the whole class will giggle and laugh together.

At this age you may notice violence figuring in play of the children. They're going to kill all the bad guys. They're going to cut off the head of someone who doesn't agree with them. They turn innocent toys into guns and start wild gunfights. This activity seems to be developmental as much as cultural. It is a stage, but you can't ignore it or the child will think you approve.

Four-year-olds have a fairly extensive vocabulary and enjoy playing in larger groups. They also can negotiate with one another. They will often work out their own differences and come up with ways to share without needing the teacher's intervention.

WHAT CAN YOU DO?

Four-year-olds need adults who have a high energy level, a sense of humor, and a love for pretend play. They need adults who don't mind lots of noise and activity.

Set limits in the classroom. Because four-year-olds have such boundless energy, they need help in knowing when it's okay to be rowdy and when they must settle down. They respond to a schedule and to rules that are repeated often. Make a large wall poster with blocks of color showing your class schedule. Learning center time might be yellow; cleanup could be green; together time might be blue; and so forth. As you frequently call their attention to the chart, children will learn the rhythm of your class time and will respond appropriately.

Help four-year-olds use suitable language. If thwarted, they may start calling you or the other children names. "We don't use those words in our class" may be all you need to say. If that admonition is not effective, a short time-out may be necessary. Teach children other words to use to express their anger. "I'm so mad I could pop." "I'm frustrated because it was my turn."

Use humor to deal with tense times. Use nonsense syllables, rhyming, making funny faces. Because four-year-olds respond so readily to humor, they will often dissolve in giggles and then be ready to move on to something else.

Plan activities and times of imaginative play. Four-year-olds like to dress up and act out stories or to act out the way they would respond to situations. When their play includes violent solutions, such as cutting off the bad guys' heads, explain that "We don't like fighting in our class." Rely on their imaginations to come up with better solutions. Ask, "How can you help the bad guys turn into good guys?"

Four-year-olds are ready for cooperative projects. They enjoy working side by side and can create a mural for the classroom, each talking about what he is doing and commenting on his neighbor's work.

Give four-year-olds opportunities to flex their larger muscles. Use fingerplays and stories with body movement; plan times of stretching, moving to music, and (if possible) outside play.

Resting time is equally important, though resting is hard for four-year-olds. Rely once more on their interest in imaginative play to help with resting activities. Letting a four-year-old lie on the floor and imagine herself running through lots of red and yellow and blue flowers can be one way to encourage her to rest.

Balance active and quiet times in the four-year-old classroom. Having large pillows to sink into and read a book or listen to a tape is just as important as having blocks with which to build.

✔ How Do You Nurture Faith in Four-Year-Olds?

Four-year-olds are beginning to gain a sense of the larger community. Church is now not just my room but also other people's rooms. Reinforce this recognition, helping four-year-olds know that all of us together all called Christians.

Four-year-olds are also beginning to show more interest in others. They respond with interest and concern to stories of children in other places who may not have the food or shelter or clothing they need.

Give four-year-olds opportunities to participate in bringing food, toys, or money for children who need it. They will do so willingly.

Four-year-olds see Jesus as a loving person. The stories that show his love and concern for others are important to them. Since they are also learning to live together in the classroom, tell them those stories told by Jesus that help us know how to live together.

It is also important to continue to help children see God as Creator. They enjoy activities outside and are fascinated with leaves, insects, rocks, and shells. Encourage them often to join in saying thanks to God for all these things.

Four-year-olds are able to repeat stories and verses from the Bible. They see the Bible as a special book that contains stories about Jesus and words about God. In retelling Bible stories, their imaginations take flight and they add wonderful conversations between Mary and Joseph or Jesus and Zacchaeus.

As an adult, continue to be the window through which children see a loving and accepting God. If in the midst of the wild, exuberant behavior of four-year-olds you show joyful acceptance of the way they are growing, they will feel that God too approves.

Expect many questions about God from four-year-olds. Just as they try to understand the world logically, they also try to figure out how God works. I remember my nephew Jonathan asking my sister if God was on the lights at church. Later, as they drove home, he asked if God was on the wheels of their car. He was trying to figure out the meaning of the words *God is everywhere.*

Listen to the questions posed by children. Answer honestly and with short answers. It's perfectly acceptable to say "I don't know." It's also fine to say "Some people think . . . .What do you think?" Accept their explanations and don't spend time correcting what to you seems wrong.

KINDERGARTNERS

Kindergarten children are mostly five-year-olds with some six-year-olds mixed in. Although children at this age are still growing and changing rapidly, the changes may not be as obvious as in the early years. Whether they are five or six, kindergartners still are not reading on their own or experiencing first grade schooling. They are still looking forward to the time when they are part of "big school." They feel both anticipation and fear as they think about growing up.

When Chris, my stepson, finished kindergarten, he said to me,

"I'm scared of first grade." "What scares you?" I asked. "Well," he said, "in first grade you have to sit at a desk and write and read, and you don't get to work in centers." As a last attempt to claim early childhood, he often said that summer, "You know, I'm not old enough to read yet." And yet he had been expressing an interest in reading for the previous two years.

At times, five- and six-year-olds may slip back into earlier behaviors. They may talk baby talk or may want to be read to as they were when they were younger. The purpose of this regressive behavior is partly to gain attention. It's also one way of dealing with some of the fear of growing up.

In spite of their fears, five- and six-year-olds are interested in school-related activities. They like to use pencils and enjoy writing. They ask adults to spell out words so that they can write the letters. They enjoy pretending to do schoolwork. They like trying to read; and many can read, at least by the end of the year.

Kindergartners are interested in the larger world. They like studying about and meeting firefighters, police officers, mail carriers, carpenters, ministers, nurses, doctors, and persons with other occupations, especially if those workers wear a uniform of some type. Kindergartners enjoy pretend play about these people, and such play is often elaborate.

Five- and six-year-olds are self-starters. They will think of something to do and then do it. They will decide to draw a picture of a house and then will draw it without any suggestion from you.

Although children in kindergarten are still active, they are calmer than four-year-olds. They are even tempered, dependable, and thoughtful; and they enjoy being taught.

Many kindergartners become perfectionists when working on their projects. They are eager to please and want to do things well. It isn't unusual to see kindergartners start and restart an art project, then not be satisfied with what they have done—especially if they are trying to copy a teacher-made model. They may become frustrated and unhappy about what they perceive as a lack of perfection.

Five- and six-year-olds have a longer attention span than younger children. They are much more likely to stay with a few activities than to flit from one to another. They love responsibility and can help with cleanup, classroom tasks, and planning.

Kindergartners also have a keener sense of time than younger children. Although they still can't tell time, they do recognize when it is time for different activities. They anticipate activities and look forward to next week or next month when something special will happen.

Most five- and six-year-olds would rather play with others than by themselves. Friends are important to them, and best friends can change often.

Five-year-olds are active and would rather run than walk or skip and jump than sit still. They love music and moving to music, making up their own dances or following a leader.

The language of five- and six-year-olds exceeds their understanding. They often use words in ways that amuse adults, putting words they understand in the place of words they don't. Thus, "Round yon virgin" becomes Round John Virgin.

WHAT CAN YOU DO?

Plan activities that deal with time and the calendar. Talk about God's gift of time and about the predictability of time and the seasons. This age level is the perfect one to make Advent calendars or Lenten calendars and to count off days to Christmas or Easter. Make use of stopwatches and timers to mark the beginning and ending of activities.

Help your class explore the world of your community and your church. Invite members of the congregation who are in uniformed professions to come in uniform to visit your class.

Plan times for discussion. Five- and six-year-olds have lots of ideas and love to talk. They know by now that if they wait, they too will have a turn and will patiently wait for each person in class to have a say.

Make use of school activities. Five- and six-year-olds can do dot-to-dots and pencil mazes and can fill in simple words. But do not confine class activities to those that can be done with pencil and paper. Kindergartners are still active and need time to use their bodies and to stretch their muscles. Balance sitting activities with games, walks, outside play, and creative movement.

As always, set limits in your classroom. Five- and six-year-olds want to know that they can depend on adults who care for them. They see this care reflected in you, their teacher, when you have rules that protect the rights of each child and of the class.

Let the children help in planning activities. Offer choices and let them follow through on their choices. Plan together service projects such as baking cookies, cleaning up the churchyard, or visiting a church member who has difficulty leaving home.

✔ How Do You Nurture Faith in Five- and Six-Year-Olds?

Kindergartners are loyal to their church. They see how the church celebrates special times of the year, and they love being a part of these celebrations. They also like being part of the group, and they grow by being included in meaningful ways in churchwide projects. Give them tasks and roles suited to their abilities during church cleanup days, mission projects, intergenerational studies, and worship services.

Five- and six-year-olds are religious beings. They see God as loving and caring for them. They respond through prayer in quiet times and through music in times of celebration. They take us seriously when we say that God listens to our prayers, and they talk earnestly to God through their prayers.

Jesus is important to the kindergarten child. She learns from hearing about Jesus' love and concern for people. She learns from hearing how Jesus prayed and talked with God. She learns from hearing how Jesus treated people others might not have liked.

Since friendship is important to five- and six-year-olds, they are trying to understand what a friend is. Stories of friendships in the Bible contribute to their understanding of friendship.

The Bible is a book that five- and six-year-olds know they will soon be able to read. They enjoy seeing where the stories they know are located in the Bible. They like to pick out words they know in the Bible. They can tell and retell favorite stories from the Bible and can say and sing many verses.

Use your whole body when telling kindergartners the stories of faith. Use motions, make up dances, jump and shout. Let children act out the stories of faith, adding their own dialogue to reflect their view of the story.

As their teacher, you are the model of what it means to be Christian. The children in your kindergarten class will model themselves after you, using the language you use and copying the actions you do. Although this role is an awesome responsibility, it is also a unique opportunity. When children enter first grade, they begin a slow but gradual movement from being dependent on adults to being dependent on peers. You can feel honored and humble that you serve as a model for young children and that you mirror God's love for them.

How Do You Teach?

I once was asked to teach a summer kindergarten class. At this particular church, only the young children had Sunday school. Everyone else went to worship. I was told that I would have the class by myself and that I would probably have around twelve children each Sunday. *No problem,* I thought. I had been teaching three-year-olds with three other teachers. I knew lots of activities that appealed to young children, and I was confident that I could have an exciting summer with the kindergarten class.

On the first Sunday I went in about an hour early. I wanted time to get the room set up. I carefully arranged the room in interest centers. I set out the materials needed at each area and made nametags for myself and for the children. I was ready.

At 9:30 a horde of children hit the room. In five minutes they had destroyed every interest area and were doing things I thought weren't possible with the tables and chairs. That hour was one of the longest of my life. After the parents came for the children and I cleaned up the mess, I sat down to think.

I had been used to teaching in a team, and our children had been carefully taught how to use interest centers. Now I was trying to teach a different age group by myself, using the same techniques I had used with younger children. They didn't work.

I was scared. Was I going to have to throw out all I knew and spend Sunday after Sunday that summer in a state of panic?

I learned a lot that summer. I learned that a variety of teaching techniques are available to teachers. I learned that teaching alone is different from teaching as a member of a team. I learned that I could still offer choices to the children, could still arrange the room in interest centers, could still spend one-on-one time with the children; but doing all these things took more work and more planning than they had when I was teaching as part of a team.

When you become a teacher of young children, three kinds of knowledge are important to you: knowledge of your age group, knowledge of ways young children learn, and knowledge of teaching techniques that appeal to the age group and that contribute to learning. As you acquire these three kinds of knowledge and put into practice what you learn, class time will become an enjoyable experience for both you and the children.

YOUNG CHILDREN LEARN THROUGH PLAY

The minute young children enter a classroom, the lesson for that day has begun. The time they spend exploring toys, sitting side by side working with play dough, and pretending to iron doll clothes is as important to their learning as the time they spend listening to you tell a story, saying Bible verses, and praying together. For young children play is learning.

The following chart, called the learning cone, shows how much children remember of what they are taught by methods that range from passive listening to active doing. Study this chart. Then ask yourself, *How much time do I spend talking to the children? How much time do I spend pairing my words with things children can see? How much time do I allow each week for children to be physically involved in learning?*

THE LEARNING CONE

Learner listens.	**Hear** stories, recordings	Children remember 10% of what you tell them.
Learner looks.	**See** pictures, videotapes, flannelgraph, bulletin boards	Children remember 60% of what they see.
Learner is involved.	**Do** interest centers, singing, movement, discussion, field trips	Children remember 90% of what they do.

Play is the work of childhood. Since fact and fantasy are still not distinct in the minds of young children, when they play out an activity, they are doing it. Through play, they explore the world.

Young children get involved in trying to figure out how grown men and women act. They decide what is dependable and what is not. They test gravity. They test their own abilities. They test what toys will or will not do. They figure out ways other children and adults react to situations. They explore ways to solve problems. They discover ways to share and to live together happily. Play is the vehicle for all of this testing and exploring.

As you offer young children opportunities for play, you nurture their faith. As you play with children, you show them how to interact in loving ways. You hold a doll and cuddle it and give it food and rock it. You take blocks and show children how to work together building roads for cars and trucks. You make dinner for friends. You roll the ball from one friend to another. You pretend to bandage a friend's hurt. Children watch you and learn from the ways you play with them.

Children develop moral values through their play. They act out what they hear and see about love, hope, faith, forgiveness, responsibility, sharing, and caring. They test these in play before making them a part of their responses to others.

Say again and again to yourself and to other adults, "The best learning activities I can plan for young children are those in which children play. I am teaching as much or more about the Christian faith when I take time to help a two-year-old care for a baby doll as I am when I tell my Bible story."

INTEREST CENTERS

Young children learn by having space and time to make choices for themselves. If they are engaged only in activities in which they work together at the same things at the same time and produce the same results, they do not develop the self-esteem that results from having confidence in their own capabilities.

This fact does not contradict the need for limits in the classroom. Young children need class times that are well planned and that are shaped by a consistent schedule.

That schedule should include times for children to work alone, to work in groups of two or three children, and to be with the total group. The plan that fits the schedule should allow children to make choices and should provide activities that let children succeed and feel that they are capable, creative, and loved.

The following centers are recommended for ages two through five. Equipment will differ by age group, and not every center is needed every week.

Creativity: Plan activities that use paint, play dough, scissors (not for age 2), paste or glue, crayons, markers, and paper. Using these tools, children discover that they can make many things and that what they make is good. These activities affirm the biblical understanding of the goodness of God's creation and that humans, being made in the image of God, are cocreators with God.

Blocks and Building: Plan activities that use small and large blocks, cars, trucks, planes, wooden figures of animals and people, farms, villages, and doll houses. This center teaches children to work together cooperatively. They gain pride in their building skill and in using their imagination to turn blocks into towers, churches, houses and roads. Through these activities, children explore the meaning of covenant and of working together in community, living within the laws of the classroom.

Family Living: Plan activities that use child-size refrigerators, stoves, ironing boards, and telephones; dolls and doll furniture; dress-up clothes, hats, and uniforms. In this center children explore what it means to be grown up, what it means to live together as a family, and what constitutes work and play for adults. The play you see here often mirrors home life, so it can be a great source of information and learning for you as a teacher. As children play, they act out the duties of parents; they state the values they hear in their own homes; they care for dolls in the same way they've been cared for at home. The biblical concepts of creation and covenant as well as of law and redemptive love come into play here. Children argue, then forgive; they share and do for one another, and they learn to define themselves as boys and girls through the activities that have been planned for in this center.

Books and Puzzles: Plan activities that use puzzles, games, pegs and pegboards, beads for stringing, and books. This center should include pillows to sit on or lean against and should be located in a quiet area of your room. Children can escape from hectic activities to be alone here or to be with one adult. These calming activities can help young children cope with the stress they encounter at home or in the classroom.

Music: Plan activities that use tape players, tapes or CD's, rhythm instruments, singing, and movement to music. Repetition is an important aspect of the activities in this center. These activities also affirm the creativity and uniqueness of each child and lead children into worship and praise for God.

Wonder: Plan activities that use rocks, shells, magnets, a magnifying glass, prisms, goldfish, pictures from magazines and curriculum. Activities in this center allow children to express their feelings of awe and wonder at this world and of worship for our creator God.

TEAM TEACHING

When you teach with other adults, you gain from their skills and ideas. Planning involves a give-and-take that isn't possible when you teach alone.

Team teaching also allows young children to relate to more than one adult and to feel more secure when one teacher isn't present. Young children who are used to only one teacher lose their sense of security when that teacher is absent and are not always happy and cooperative with a substitute.

Team teaching allows more flexibility for personal schedules. When a class has three teachers, if one needs time for vacation, family time, or illness, the other two insure that the class is not disrupted. In fact, many teams build into their schedules time away for each teacher. Teacher burnout occurs less frequently as a result.

Team teaching requires regular meetings to study the Bible together, to plan together, to assign responsibilities, to pool resources, and to arrange the classroom space and keep it neat and clean. Team teaching takes more planning time than teaching alone, but it also means that class responsibilities are shared and that creativity is nurtured.

If you are teaching in a team, the team needs to meet for two or three hours at the beginning of each quarter. Prior to the meeting, each team member should have read the material and should have marked points of particular interest to him or her.

During the meeting, first study the major portions of Scripture together. Talk about which ones you feel should get the greatest emphasis during the quarter. Then talk about activities that will make this Scripture interesting and important to the children in your class. Plan to have briefer weekly meetings or to have phone meetings at least once each week during the quarter.

If you are part of a team, say thanks to the Sunday school superintendent, coordinator, or education chair who helped get your team set up. If you are teaching alone, lobby for a team. If the numbers of children make it possible, you might be able to combine classes with another age group and team teach with that group's teacher.

Using Interest Centers When You Teach Alone

If you are the only teacher in a young children's class, you should provide only two or three interest centers at a time. Children will gradually learn to work with one another and will interact with one another as you visit from center to center. Some centers need your direct help. At others children can work more independently. One week you may need to be at the table with the creative art activities, supervising the use of glue. The next week you may need to be in the family living area to make a snack for the entire group.

If you teach alone, plan only one really messy or time-consuming activity each week. It could be painting, building an elaborate church together, making peanut butter and cracker sandwiches, or using the rhythm instruments. Plan for calmer activities to take place in the other areas of the room.

Before class each week, remove items you do not plan for children to use. If the cars and trucks aren't needed this week, put them away. If you don't plan to use puzzles, put them away. Rotating toys instead of using the same ones each week keeps everyone's interest high.

Even when you're seated at one center, you can guide children at other centers by your conversation. "I see that Andrew and Scott are sweeping their house, getting ready for visitors. In our story today, you'll hear how Sarah got ready for visitors."

Yes, doing so is possible; but no one should teach young children alone. Each young children's classroom should have at least two teachers. If there is only one teacher in your young children's class, you are not providing the best safety and care for that class. You need to be prepared for emergencies and for times when a child needs extra attention and care. On the next page are suggested maximum ratios of adults to children for classes of young children. Remember, the smaller the ratio, the easier to give individual children needed attention.

MAXIMUM RATIOS OF ADULTS TO CHILDREN IN CLASSES OF YOUNG CHILDREN

Age Group	Maximum Class Size	Ratio of Adults to Children
Infants	8 to 12	1 to 4 with at least 2 adults always present
Toddlers	16	1 to 6 with at least 2 adults always present
Nursery (2- and 3-year-olds)	16	1 to 8 with at least 2 adults always present
Kindergarten (4- and 5-year olds)	20	1 to 10 with at least 2 adults always present

ORGANIZING CLASS TIME

As you prepare to teach, balance quiet times with active times, individual and small group activities with large group activities. Here are three sample schedules for one-hour times:

SCHEDULE A:

9:45–10:15 Child arrival. Have children leave offerings at the worship table. Let them choose from interest center activities.

10:15–10:30 Together time. Share a story, sing a song, do fingerplays, move to music, pray together.

10:30–10:45 Group activity or choice of two activities that illustrate the story. As parents arrive, children leave from activities.

This schedule allows children to come into the class at different times and to leave at different times. Often when all the children are grouped together and parents start picking up their children, those whose parents haven't come yet cry. If children are engaged in individual activities, however, they are less likely to notice others leaving. The younger the children, the more time they need in activities of their choice and the less time in the total group. Expand time together for four- and five-year-olds, but reduce the time spent together for two-year-olds.

SCHEDULE B:

9:45–10:00   Children's assembly. All children in the department meet together for group singing, prayers, and an offering.

10:00–10:30   Interest centers. Children choose activities in centers.

10:30–10:45   Together time. Time for stories, fingerplays, praying together, or saying a litany. Children leave from the group circle.

SCHEDULE C:

9:45–10:10   Group activity. As children enter, they join the large group for name games, songs, and a story.

10:10–10:40   Interest centers. Children choose activities in interest centers.

10:40–10:45   Children come back to the total group to share what they've learned and for a departing prayer.

Schedules B and C work well if all your children arrive at about the same time and leave together.

WHAT ABOUT THE BIBLE?

3

As a Christian teacher, you want your children to have an appreciation for and a love of the Bible. You want your children to know Scripture and to be able to apply the teachings of the Bible to their daily lives. You are also aware, however, that the concepts and words of the Bible are adult words. Thus you may struggle with what to teach in the Bible and how to teach it.

The Bible is important to children because it is important to adults. I remember Chris's first Bible, a small white New Testament. He was four and couldn't read; but he carried that Bible around with him, pretending to read by saying "God" or "Amen" here and there as he turned its pages. That Bible was important to him. He had seen adults who cared for him read their Bibles, so he too wanted to read that important book.

Having a Bible in your classroom is of primary importance even though the children you teach cannot read. Children will not develop a love for the Bible if they don't see adults reading from the Bible. Whenever you tell or read a Bible story, always show the children where the story is found in the Bible.

PLEASE TOUCH

Children should be able to touch and handle the Bible in their classroom. If you say, "No, don't touch," when you use the Bible, you may stifle a child's desire to read from the Bible. Instead, let children handle the Bible, turn its pages, and pretend to read it. Doing so will prepare them for the time when they have their own Bibles and are able to read. Teach children how to care for the Bible just as you teach them how to care for other books.

Young children first learn about the Bible as a book. They are aware that the Bible is a special book and that it tells stories of Jesus. They should know that the Bible in their Sunday school room is the same book as the Bible they have at home. They can understand some simply told stories from the Bible that relate to their own experiences.

Children this age love stories and will listen to them as long as the stories aren't too long. Because young children's sense of time and space is limited, they aren't concerned about when or where these stories happened. They enjoy the stories for the moment. They need to hear stories about God's love and care, about Jesus and how he lived, and about Jesus' love for children.

At four, five, and six, children have a longer attention span. They begin to discuss the Bible stories they've been told and to add their opinions to the stories. Acting out stories from the Bible is an enjoyable way to learn for four-, five-, and six-year-olds. They like to use their imagination and will apply their imagination to the stories of the Bible. For example, they might take on the character of Mary and act out caring for the baby Jesus.

A test for choosing a Bible story for the preschool level is to ask, How does this story relate to the children's experience? If it doesn't, why tell it? There are many others to be told.

READ IT AGAIN

Children learn best through repetition. One Sunday I walked into a three-year-old classroom toward the end of the class period. The teacher was reading a book, and the children sat enthralled at her feet. The book wasn't related to the day's lesson, and after Sunday school the teacher sought me out to apologize for reading something that wasn't part of the lesson plan. She said that she had read the book to the class several weeks earlier and that since that Sunday, the children had requested that she read it week after week, not wanting to leave the classroom until they had heard that particular story again.

I assured the teacher that nothing was wrong with repeating a story again and again. By her doing so, the children learned the story thoroughly. As the story became more familiar, their minds were freed to imagine and wonder and add to the story.

Not least important was the fact that each time the teacher listened to those children and read something that they asked for, she reinforced their feelings of being loved and cared for. The words in the Bible mean little to young children without teachers and parents who live out the message of the Bible as that message relates to the young child.

YOUNG CHILDREN AND BIBLICAL KNOWLEDGE

As a young children's Sunday school teacher you may be tempted to teach your students everything you know about the Bible. This urge is fueled by your realization that educating children is an important task and by a natural desire on your part to help your students learn everything important to their faith. Relax and remember that you are simply one in a long line of teachers. Children have many years to learn what you know about the Bible.

So what can preschool children learn about the Bible, and what is appropriate to teach them? Here are a few ideas.

You can teach young children words of praise from the Bible. *Praise God* is an important phrase. We Christians spend all our lives praising and thanking God. We can start this attitude and practice of thanksgiving with our youngest children.

You can teach stories about Jesus—Jesus as a baby, Jesus as a boy who grew, Jesus as a teacher and what he taught, Jesus as a man who loved children, Jesus as a man who lived and died and lived again. Teach these stories simply, using few words.

You can teach stories of people in the Bible who loved God. Choose stories that have some meaning to a child and tell them often. You can tell of Abraham's moving, because children have experienced moving and understand what moving means. You can tell about the birth of babies, because all children have been babies and many have new babies in their families. You can tell of Jeremiah and Isaiah because they prayed and talked with God just as you do.

You can teach about God. Starting with God as creator and talking about the world God created, you can begin sharing ways you care for the world God created. You can share stories of how God loves people because you have already laid the foundation for the children's understanding that God loves us. You can tell children about biblical people who helped others know God's love.

The preschool years are the times to build familiarity with Bible stories and verses, choosing just a few at first. Remember, children have many years to learn all the stories of the Bible.

WHAT ABOUT MEMORIZING?

Children memorize all the time. That's the way they learn numbers, their ABC's, their address, and songs from children's television programs. For children, memorization is a way of life. The question is not, then, Should children memorize Bible verses and stories? The appropriate question is, How do you help children learn words and stories from the Bible in ways that bring peace, love, joy, and excitement to both you and the child?

I remember two types of memorization from my childhood. One made me fearful and angry. It was typified by what we called sword drills. Holding our Bibles in one hand, we stood in a line and waited anxiously as the teacher called out a verse. We then thumbed furiously through our Bibles and stepped forward when we found the verse. Being the last one to find the verse was like being the last one chosen for a team at recess. For others, the thrill of competition may have sparked a love and joy for learning. For me, the fear of being last did nothing to make me feel joyful about learning Scripture. This kind of learning activity set up a classroom situation that labeled some children winners and others losers. Make sure that the methods you use to help children learn Scripture are designed in such a way that every child is a winner.

I also remember learning words from the Bible out of a great love and respect for my teacher. In the third grade our entire class learned the story of Jesus' birth from Luke 2. We learned it together, saying it in unison week after week, until together we could recite all of it for the Christmas pageant. Because we were learning and saying it as a group, if one of us faltered at any one point, the rest of the group kept going and we could pick up at the next point. What a sense of accomplishment all of us had the night of the pageant.

I still close my eyes and recite Luke 2 every Christmas. I love those passages of Scripture, and I know my love of them comes from learning those words as a child.

Words and stories stored deep in our memories become part of us. They help us act in ways that are harmonious with the words. They give us peace and hope when we are fearful. Memorization instills a knowledge of Scripture in such a way that it can never be forgotten. Memorization frees us from the progression of words and allows us to go deep into the meaning of the Scripture.

This kind of knowing doesn't happen in one day or one month or one year, however. We start young children on this journey of knowing, and it grows as they grow.

As a teacher, you hope that every time you help children learn words from the Bible, they experience joy of learning, pride of accomplishment, and love of Scripture. Use the following do's and don'ts about memorization to guide your teaching.

MEMORIZATION DO'S

Memorization is an ongoing process. As you plan your lesson each week, be sure you've included time to help children learn Scripture, songs, and prayers. As children learn words from the Bible, prayers, hymns, creeds, and responses, they feel included in worship at home and in church.

Know the characteristics of your age group. Think through what you can generally expect from them (see the appropriate section in Chapter 1). Children who do not yet have an extensive vocabulary cannot memorize and retell a lengthy Bible story, Bible verse, or story song. Often, though, even very young children with limited vocabularies can and do learn motions and movements to stories, verses, and songs. Doing so is their way of remembering the words and can be as valuable as saying or singing the words.

Make memorization fun. Encourage the learning of Scripture through motions, songs, acting out the verses, saying the stories or verses together as a group, using verses for prayers, hiding words around the room and having a hunt to put the words back together in order, drawing pictures of the stories and verses, listening to a tape telling the verse or story, using puppets and flannelboard figures.

Pick out one or two verses and one story each quarter that you want the children to learn. Spend several weeks on each passage. Sunday after Sunday use the activities listed in the previous paragraph to help the children learn these verses and stories.

Pick passages that are reinforced by the curriculum and by worship services. Verses learned in isolation from the stories and rituals of the church are usually not remembered long.

Once your children have learned a verse or story, use it. Invite parents to come and listen to the children tell or act out a favorite Bible story. Make posters, bookmarks, and plaques that contain the words of the verses. Have memory times as part of your class, letting children tell what they remember from past lessons. Visit adult classes or other children's classes and share your stories.

Finally, reward the children with praise and class celebrations.

MEMORIZATION DON'TS

Singling children out one by one to say the verse of the day can strike fear in the heart of a child even if he does know the verse. Being singled out puts pressure on the child to perform for the sake of performing, not for the love of learning the verse or story. This activity also sets up some children to be successful and others to be failures. In Sunday school you want all your children to be successful so that they grow in self-confidence and in the assurance of God's love and care.

Making fun of children who can't remember is never acceptable. You may say to yourself, *Why, I would never make fun of a child.* But unfortunately you do it in subtle ways. For example, it happens when you say, "We'll give Jonathan another week. It takes him a long time to remember." It happens when you say, "Michelle is still too little to be able to do what the rest of you are doing." Children feel you are making fun of them when you say, "This is an easy verse. Everyone can remember it." If they really can't, they feel inferior and stupid. Use great care in the words you use to introduce and encourage memorization.

Asking children to remember a different verse or story each week is not an effective way to help them memorize. It takes time to learn stories and verses. Children forget, particularly if they've heard something only once or twice. And a lot happens from one Sunday to the next. They need to hear stories and verses again and again.

Rewarding with trinkets or prizes is ineffective. Contrary to what you might think, trinkets or prizes actually devalue the learning of Scripture. Children quickly learn to value the prizes instead of the learning. And they learn just as quickly that the value of these prizes isn't very great. Having class celebrations, clapping for one another, singing a happy song together, and hugging are more lasting rewards.

Don't choose stories or verses that are irrelevant to the experiences of a young child. Our goal is always to lead the child to a growing, living relationship with God. Choose words and stories that help develop this relationship.

APPROPRIATE SCRIPTURE FOR MEMORIZATION

Scripture in denominational curriculum resources for young children is selected for its appropriateness for the age level. Each quarter read through all the material for both the teacher and the children. Select two verses that seem to best relate to your students. Choose one Bible story to learn during the quarter. As you go through the weekly lessons, you may introduce other verses and stories; but you should come back to these two verses and story often.

Be sure to let parents know your focus for the quarter. Post a note outside the door of your classroom. Invite parents to be a part of your class so that they can hear what their children are learning. Call attention to suggestions in the curriculum for learning at home.

Following are some Scriptures that can be learned by young children. Use them when they relate to what your class is studying for the quarter.

A G E S 3 – 4

Verses

"We love, because God first loved us." (1 John 4:19, adapted)

"Jesus said, 'Love one another.'" (John 13:34*a*, adapted)

"A friend loves at all times." (Proverbs 17:17)

"Be kind to one another." (Ephesians 4:32)

"God cares about you." (1 Peter 5:7, adapted)

"God is love." (1 John 4:8)

"It is good to give thanks to God." (Psalm 92:1, adapted)

Stories

Abraham and Sarah have a baby (Genesis 21:1-8)

Jesus' birth (Luke 2)

Jesus makes friends with Zacchaeus (Luke 19:1-10)

A G E S 5 – 6

Verses

"Stop and consider the wondrous works of God." (Job 37:14)

"This is the day that the Lord has made; let us rejoice and be glad in it." (Psalm 118:24)

"I was glad when they said to me, 'Let us go to the house of the Lord.'" (Psalm 122:1)

"And now faith, hope, and love abide, these three; and the greatest of these is love." (1 Corinthians 13:13)

"Jesus said, 'Love the Lord your God with all your heart.
. . . Love your neighbor as yourself.'" (Luke 10:27, adapted)

"Jesus said, "Let the little children come to me, and do not stop them, for it is to such as these that the kingdom of heaven belongs.'" (Matthew 19:14)

"In the beginning God created the heavens and the earth." (Genesis 1:1, adapted)

"Love the Lord your God with all your heart, and with all your soul, and with all your might." (Deuteronomy 6:5)

Stories

God created the earth (Genesis 1 and 2)

Jonathan is a friend to David (1 Samuel 20)

Jesus' birth (Luke 2 and Matthew 2)

The good Samaritan (Luke 10:30-35)

Jesus and the children (Mark 10:13-16)

How Do You Nurture Faith?

When Chris, my stepson, was a school-age child, Sunday morning conversations often began with "Why do we have to go to church? We don't have to go to church in Texas. Why do we have to go here?" Chris lived with his mom and stepdad in Texas during the school year and with us in Tennessee during the summer. Helping Chris regain the habit of going to church each summer when he came to live with us was a struggle. Every first Sunday of his time with us I sent up a little prayer that the teachers in his class would have such good activities planned that the following Sunday would begin without a struggle. And frequently Chris did have good experiences that made him feel better about church attendance.

But his questions always made me think hard about my own values. Why was it important to go to Sunday school and worship? What did we get from these experiences that was different from experiencing God, say, on the riverbank? What did Chris gain from Sunday school classmates and teachers that he didn't gain through home worship and prayer times with us?

And the questions continued when I became the parent of an infant. What did Benjamin get from Sunday school besides the latest cold or virus? What difference did it make for a child of less than one year to be with other young children in the church nursery and with the family during worship services?

If I had believed that the only things my children were getting on Sunday morning were cute crafts and baby-sitting, getting everyone dressed, fed, and out of the house early on Sunday mornings wouldn't have been worth the struggle. But I do believe important things happened for my children at church on Sunday mornings and in weekday programs too.

Every activity the teachers planned was grounded in the belief that they were sharing their faith and providing opportunities for my children and other children to grow in the knowledge and love of God. What we did at home was strengthened and reinforced in the larger community at church. Chris is no longer a child, and Benjamin is no longer an infant; but my hope for them and for all other children continues to be that they feel welcomed into the church and into a faith in God.

CREATING A WELCOMING ENVIRONMENT

Think for a minute about receiving an invitation. Can you remember getting one that was particularly exciting for you? Perhaps it was an invitation to a party or to a gathering of family and friends. It was probably personally addressed to you. You probably knew the person issuing the invitation.

An exciting invitation carries the promise of fellowship with people you know and enjoy. It usually promises something fun to do. And it often signals an important event—a birthday, a christening or baptism, a wedding, a graduation.

Children should feel the same excitement when they are invited into the faith. What does this challenge mean for you as a teacher of young children? Your first goal should be to prepare yourself and your classroom so that young children feel wanted, accepted, and excited to be with you.

Let's think again about young children and what we know of their wants and needs. Children from infancy through six years of age need teachers who are committed to being with them for most of the Sundays in the year. Young children build trust in their teachers and are slow to accept a substitute. When adults pop in and out of teaching throughout the year, children learn not to count on Mrs. Lambert or Mr. Reuben. Because young children form opinions about God and Jesus based on their experiences with adults, the inconsistency of their teachers can cause them to view God as inconsistent and arbitrary, not to be trusted.

Children from infancy through six years of age need teachers to be in the classroom before they arrive. When children arrive first, teachers have a hard time recapturing and redirecting the interests of those children who have already begun activities that suit their imaginations with little regard for the purposes planned by the absent teacher.

Routine is important to the development of trust in children from infancy through six years. Knowing their routines in church allows young children to trust both the teacher and the environment. From infancy through six years of age, children identify *church* with "my room at Sunday school or nursery school." Their space is important to them. They need equipment that is appropriate to their size and a room that welcomes them, is safe and clean, and reflects their personalities. Since *room* means church and *church* means God, the rooms they learn in are essential to making children feel invited into faith.

Children from infancy through six years of age are establishing their own identity. They respond to being called by name and enjoy hearing their own name and seeing things they have made. They love seeing pictures of themselves and those they know. They respond when adults call them by name, when adults remember things about them, and when adults show that they enjoy being around them.

Think about the environment you provide for the children in your class. Does it help them feel welcomed and secure? Do you create an environment where children can respond to the invitation to grow as faithful disciples?

TEACHING AS JESUS TAUGHT

Jesus taught by constantly pointing to the nature of God and the kind of life that led to close communion with God. Those who listened to his teaching were invited into fellowship and partnership with God.

Jesus taught through stories. Instead of giving a short answer to a question, Jesus said, "Let me tell you a story." As he told the story, he drew listeners into the story. Points were made in the story so that his listeners could say, "Oh, yes. Now I understand."

Jesus taught by using the everyday experiences of his listeners. He didn't try to tell stories or to use examples from other lands, other times, or other types of people. He drew upon occurrences and activities the people he was speaking to saw and did daily. He used examples of baking bread, making wine, tending sheep, searching for lost coins; and he drew upon the imagery of weddings, olive trees, and mustard seeds. All of these examples and images made sense to the people of Jesus' time. They knew exactly what he was talking about.

When you tell stories and plan activities for young children, you can teach as Jesus taught by using illustrations from the everyday lives of your children. For example, while caring for sheep may not be something your children experience, they do know how to care for pets or for younger brothers and sisters.

Jesus also taught through example. His life showed what it meant to be close to God. His followers saw him read Scripture, pray to God, and make decisions based on his understanding of God's will. Jesus didn't just talk faith; he lived it.

Jesus taught through repetition. Do you remember Jesus' conversation with Peter after the Resurrection? Jesus asked Peter to "feed my sheep." He didn't ask only once, but three times. As Jesus repeated the question, it grew in power and meaning. And Peter was much more likely to remember the question because of hearing it three times.

As you teach young children, do you hurry through lesson after lesson, never stopping to repeat stories, songs, activities? Stop and say to yourself, "These things are important enough to say and do again and again." Through repetition, children remember and learn. Jesus practiced repetition. So can you.

Jesus focused on the individual. Think about his conversation with the woman at the well. He listened to her, responded to her, and took time to answer her questions. Think about Zacchaeus. Jesus didn't say to all the crowd, "I want to eat dinner with all of you." Jesus focused on Zacchaeus, saying, "I want to eat dinner with you, Zacchaeus, because I think you are a child of God."

LISTENING TO CHILDREN

How can you focus on individuals when you are responsible for a class full of children? One way is to make sure that you include in your lesson plan times to listen to your students. It's important to have time for the children to talk about their experiences and feelings. If you ask only questions with set answers, you have no opportunity to listen to your children.

Think about the story of the lost sheep. After telling the story, if you only say to children, "How many sheep were lost?" "What did the shepherd do?" "Where did he put the sheep that were not lost?" you have no opportunity to listen to the children as individuals. If you ask instead, "What do you think it felt like to be the sheep that was lost? Have you ever been lost? Please tell me about it," then you can really listen to your children.

Jesus taught in ways that invited persons into a loving and demanding relationship with God. His examples are our legacy as teachers of the faith.

SHARING YOUR FAITH

Sometimes your teaching may feel like merely performing a duty, filling a space, or getting through until the bell. When those times come, remember that you have a faith to share, children with whom to share it, and a time and place provided by your church. When you focus on sharing your faith, your time becomes valuable and important.

By teaching as a faithful Christian, you invite children to see in words and example the faith of biblical persons, of persons in your church and community, and of persons in your class. You invite children to express freely their own faith by talking with them, by teaching them actions that reflect that faith, and by inviting their friends to be with them in Sunday school and worship. You help the next generation live out their faith and teach it to others through words and examples.

How can you do the best job of sharing your faith so that children grow in their commitment and ability to be disciples? First seek to learn as much about the children you teach as possible. Know their interests; their ways of learning; and their ways of looking at the Bible, God, and the church.

Teaching for faith means helping young children build faith upon the foundation of basic trust. Be regular in your teaching attendance. We have discussed how the regular presence of a teacher can build trust in children.

Trust can also be built by following through on promises. If you say to a child, "Elizabeth is using the paints now. You may use them later, Malik," it is important for Malik to have the opportunity later to use the paints he wants.

You also build trust as you talk often about God and about what God means to you. When you say, "Look at the red and gold leaves. Aren't they beautiful? Thank you, God, for leaves," you build trust in a God who cares.

NURTURING SELF-IDENTITY

In the classroom, do you provide choices for children so that they do not always have to do what everyone else is doing? Do you encourage children to ask questions, and do you give honest but short answers to those questions? Do you provide crafts that the child can do herself rather than your having to put them together for her? Do you use praise and recognize positive behavior rather than focusing on disruptive behavior? Do you talk about and treat each child as a child of God?

As you provide experiences that nurture the identity of each child you teach, you are teaching that God loves each person. You foster self-identity through the choices you offer, through positive experiences, through activities that challenge but still allow your students to succeed, and through the opportunities you give them to both talk and listen.

Children like to try out new ideas, new activities. When you allow experimentation, less-than-perfect (by adult standards) work, and answers that show how they think, you can say to them, "Gosh, you are pretty wonderful." Telling children that God loves them and accompanying this statement with experiences that build a positive self-image lead children into faith and help them feel confident about talking about their faith.

BUILDING POSITIVE RELATIONSHIPS

Building positive relationships with young children enables you to share your faith. Young children love and care for adults. They see adults as all powerful and all knowing; in fact, they see adults as very much like God. God for them is like their mommy or daddy who cares for them. They look to parents and leaders as models and mimic the behavior they see. They want to be with adults and to be involved in activities they see adults they love doing. They ask questions and trust adults to share their faith through honest answers.

Inviting children to a life as a disciple of Jesus calls for action. They will follow your example as you try to obey God and treat others justly. Even though young children are egocentric—interested in their own lives and those of immediate family and friends—you can build a foundation for children to begin thinking about the broader aspects of faith, such as mission and stewardship, by talking about their own wants and needs.

Children know what they like and need. If you begin there, you can encourage children to sympathize with other children who need toys, food, clothes, or a home but don't have them. You can plan for projects that encourage children in their concern for others. You can collect money, collect toys, bring food, make cards, donate mittens. Your commitment to the teachings of Jesus is seen in these activities. Being disciples takes seriously the task of helping children live in ways that show faith.

WHAT ABOUT PHYSICAL NEEDS?

The space where teaching and learning takes place is important. The way a room looks reflects our feelings about the importance of the people who gather in that space and the importance of what happens in that space. Take a walk through all the rooms of your church. Which ones show the most care? Which ones always look clean? Which ones are free of clutter; have up-to-date bulletin boards; and have no old, broken equipment?

Unfortunately, space for children is often marred by dirt, broken toys, cluttered cabinets, last season's bulletin board, and messy walls. It suggests to parents and children that what goes on in this space is of little value. Contrast this scene with the appearance of the sanctuary or the church parlor. Usually these spaces show care and good upkeep. The message that is reflected is that what goes on in these spaces is more important than what goes on in the nursery and children's rooms. The implicit message is that adults are more valued than are children.

All space in a church should be well maintained and clean. If you believe that what happens in the rooms of your church building is important, then you should be good stewards of that space.

Not every church has space or money to provide sophisticated equipment and toys for children. It is more important to make sure what you do have in the classroom is in good condition and is kept clean. Cleaning every classroom from top to bottom at least every six months, throwing out items that clutter the room, toys that are broken, and back issues of curriculum, is a good practice. Children and parents, as well as teachers and other leaders, need to be involved in such cleanup times.

SAFETY CONCERNS FOR INFANT AND TODDLER ROOMS

1. No electrical or drapery cords should hang within children's reach.

2. Electrical outlets should be covered with a safety plug or concealed behind stationary furniture. If you are building, plan to install outlets forty-four inches above the floor.

3. Floor rugs should be secured to prevent slipping.

4. Draperies and wall hangings should not be made of flammable fabrics or fiberglass.

5. Fire extinguishers and a fire escape plan should be prominently visible in the room.

6. Windows and mirrors should be of shatterproof materials or protected with screens.

7. Plants, if present, should hang out of reach of children to prevent their chewing on leaves.

8. All furniture should be stable and tip-proof.

SAFETY GUIDELINES FOR NURSERY WORKERS

1. Pick up toys that people are likely to trip over.

2. Lock up medicines, cleaning materials, and plastic bags.

3. Check toys frequently for broken edges, parts that could be swallowed, and loose pieces.

4. Make sure that your hands are dry when handling babies.

5. Feed babies in sitting position to prevent choking.

6. Ask parents to send plastic bottles only.

7. Keep a list of parents' names and locations during the time babies are in the nursery.

8. Remove bumper pads and mobiles from cribs when babies are able to stand and use them for climbing.

CLEANING RECOMMENDATIONS FOR INFANT AND TODDLER ROOMS

To ensure the cleanest possible conditions, clean infant and toddler rooms frequently. The more frequently these rooms are used, the more frequently items need to be cleaned. Churches that have Parents Day Out or daycare need to clean the infant and toddler rooms daily. A washer and dryer can be a good investment for these programs. If these rooms are used on Sundays only, consider these recommendations.

- Weekly vacuuming of the floor, especially the feeding area, and damp mopping of spill areas

- Weekly cleaning of the most frequently used equipment, such as changing tables, infant seats, and highchairs

- Periodic cleaning of *all* equipment and immediate washing of any item that becomes sticky

- Weekly washing of all toys in a mild solution of bleach and water.

- Putting a washable blanket on the floor under younger babies who are likely to spit up

- Changing diapers as soon as they become wet or soiled

- Carefully cleaning the baby during diaper changes

- Washing hands before and after diaper changes

- Careful washing of eating utensils if children are fed

- Washing baby's hands before and after finger feeding (giving crackers, cookies, and so forth)

- Asking parents to bring a change of clothing for their child

- Changing the child's clothes if they become wet or soiled

- Changing bed linens regularly

- Changing bed linens immediately if they become soiled

- Having a sick-baby policy or an isolation room for children who become sick while staying in the nursery

Following are lists of common equipment and material needs for each age level of young children. If your church is unable to provide every item listed, determine which items are the most essential and appropriate. As you do so, remember that rooms for the youngest children may be the most important rooms in your church. For many young parents, the care their children receive determines their choice of a church home.

Rooms for infants and toddlers should be furnished so that the child's needs to be fed, kept dry, and cuddled can easily be met. Keep in mind that what children are learning most at this age is that church is a place where they are welcome; where adults love and care for them; and where they can play, explore, and grow.

THE ROOM FOR INFANTS

ENVIRONMENT

- 35 square feet of floor space per child (If this room is not used for Parent's Day Out or daycare, 20 square feet may be enough; but remember that space is needed for early walkers.)

- At least partial carpeting or skidproof area rugs

- Adjustable lighting that can be varied for sleeping, eating, and play times

- Light or neutral walls with wall hangings or pictures in cheerful primary colors (red, yellow, and blue)

EQUIPMENT AND MATERIALS

- Adult-size rocking chairs with high backs and large arms, preferably with fixed rockers to prevent injury to crawling babies

- Cribs with slats less than 2 3/8 inches apart and firm mattresses

- Changing tables

- Infant seats, a playpen with tight mesh or closely spaced slats, a sturdy automatic swing

- A cabinet, equipped with a safety latch, for the following supplies

- Soap, wipes, tissues, disposable gloves, first-aid kit, crib sheets and blankets, extra diapers, paper towels, bags for diaper disposal, water-bleach mixture in a spray bottle for disinfecting, tape and a marking pen for identifying a child's belongings, health and safety records, curriculum materials, cradle roll

- Crib toys that can easily be cleaned: mobiles, rattles, soft toys, unbreakable mirrors

- Sink with hot and cold running water

- Refrigerator

- Bottle warmer (Do not use a microwave oven to warm bottles.)

- Cubbyholes for babies' bags and wraps

- Closet for workers' supplies

- Bathroom for adults

- Highchairs

- Cassette tape player or CD player

THE ROOM FOR TODDLERS (ONE- TO TWO-YEAR-OLDS)

ENVIRONMENT

- 35 square feet of floor space per child

- At least partial carpeting or skidproof area rugs

- Good lighting

- Light or neutral walls with wall hangings or pictures in cheerful primary colors (red, yellow, and blue) hung at toddlers' eye level

- Unbreakable mirrors hung at toddlers' eye level

- Minimal furniture so that children have maximum room for playing

EQUIPMENT AND MATERIALS

- Crib and playpen as needed

- Cabinet, equipped with a safety latch, for the following supplies

- Soap, wipes, tissues, disposable gloves, first-aid kit, crib sheets and blankets, extra diapers and training pants, paper cups, paper towels, bags for diaper disposal, water-bleach mixture in a spray bottle for disinfecting, tape and marking pen for identifying a child's belongings, health and safety records, curriculum materials, cradle roll

- Open shelves for toys

- Sink at adult level with hot and cold running water
- Low book or work table
- Two or three child-size chairs
- Rocking chairs for adults
- Cubbyholes or other space for children's personal belongings
- Toys that can be easily cleaned: soft dolls, stuffed animals, push-pull toys, balls
- Cloth or heavy cardboard books
- Manipulative toys: six- to eight-piece puzzles, nesting blocks, a ball with holes for inserting blocks in a variety of shapes
- Cassette tape or CD player
- Rhythm instruments
- Climbing equipment and big-muscle toys such as a rocking boat and tunnel
- Low sink and toilet for children

THE ROOM FOR TWO-YEAR-OLDS THROUGH KINDERGARTNERS

ENVIRONMENT

- 35 square feet of floor space per child
- At least partial carpeting or skidproof area rugs
- Light or neutral walls with wall hangings or pictures in cheerful primary colors (red, yellow, and blue)
- Good lighting and ventilation

EQUIPMENT AND MATERIALS

- Tables and chairs in sizes to fit the age of the child (remembering that children at this age do not have to sit in chairs to do activities)
- Low open shelves for toys
- Cubbyholes for storing personal belongings
- A low rod for hanging children's wraps

- Bathrooms adjacent to the room

- Sinks with hot and cold running water

- Flat pictures or posters placed at children's eye level

- Worship table

- *For creative artwork:* painting easels, paint, large brushes, smocks, paper (newsprint or butcher paper, construction paper, fingerpaint paper), paste, glue, play dough, modeling clay, cookie cutters, rolling pins, blunt-tipped scissors, crayons, markers

- *For family life:* dolls, doll bed, bedding, and doll clothes; child-size stove, sink, refrigerator, table, chairs, dishes, pots and pans, brooms, mop, iron, and ironing board; dress-up clothes; stethoscope; hats; telephones (at least two)

- *For blocks and block play:* large hollow blocks, solid building blocks, cars, trucks, boats, airplanes, wooden animals and people, villages, farms, houses

- *Manipulative toys:* wooden puzzles, pegboards with large pegs, light-up boards with pegs, balls

- *Big-muscle toys (need at least one):* rocking boat, tunnel, climbing dome, indoor slide

- *Sand table:* muffin tins, cake pans, sieves, cups

- *Water table:* eggbeater, bubble pipe, squeeze bottles, cups, funnels

- *For music activities:* cassette or CD player, tapes and/or CD's, autoharp, rhythm instruments

- *For science or nature activities:* shells, rocks, magnifying glass, prisms, magnets, fish, class pets such as hamsters

- *Books:* Bible storybooks and good picture books

ABOUT SPACE FOR THE YOUNG CHILD

Children need open space as much as they need space filled with materials. They need space in which to jump and move and stretch. Such activities are part of God's plan for them to grow. Young children's rooms need to reflect that need.

If you have small rooms with lots of children, remove furniture. Plan to do activities seated on the floor or standing around tables rather than sitting at tables. Tables and chairs take up the most space in young children's rooms, and they probably are the most unnecessary items in the room.

Your space should be arranged to encourage children to make choices. It should encourage children's curiosity and should help them become excited about exploring the space. It should provide activities and places for them to try out new things, to use their bodies, and to nurture their self-concept.

If the lists of materials and equipment appear to be overwhelming, remember that they describe the ideal situation. But even if you don't have money to provide everything on the lists, there may be low-cost or no-cost ways of acquiring many of the items. Your congregation may include members who are excellent carpenters and who can build family life items, blocks, shelves, and pegboards for you. Small plastic swimming pools make excellent water and sand tables. Use your imagination. Remember also that many families with grown children may have some of the listed items at home and are no longer using them.

Garage and yard sales are good sources for children's toys and equipment. Inspect any used equipment carefully for broken pieces, however. If an item is broken, refuse it graciously. Use only items that are in good condition to ensure the safety of every child in your care. Don't keep any toys or equipment that you would not use with your own child.

Your room teaches your children. It says, "Welcome. I offer many ways for you to learn and to grow. I offer a space where you will learn to live together and to know what it means to be a Christian. I am here for you. I will be your room and your space at church because you are important—a child of God."

How Do You Plan?

One spring some friends of ours took a vacation to visit friends in another state. They had looked forward to being away from work and left anticipating a great time.

When they returned, I asked how they had enjoyed their vacation. "We had some problems," was the reply. Further conversation revealed that they had planned for the time they would be with friends but hadn't planned their travel time. Without a travel plan, they argued about where to stop, how long to stay, and how far to travel each day. Their unplanned time caused more stress than if they had stayed at home.

Planning is important to most undertakings, and it is especially important in teaching young children. You plan in order to insure the best experience for the children you teach and the best experience for yourself as their teacher. Planning gives form to your time together. Planning gives direction and purpose to your activities. Planning helps you measure your progress and determine what your next steps should be.

When you plan, bring together information about the children in your class, about yourself as a teacher, about your teaching space, about the resources you use, and about the available time you have to be together. It's important each time you plan either to write out this information or to keep these factors in mind, reviewing them from time to time.

Planning for the Year

When you begin your teaching year, first list what you hope the children in your class will know or experience by the end of the year. Write down these hopes as objectives. Objectives answer the questions who, what, when, and where. They say who you are teaching, what you want to be learned or experienced, when you want this learning to happen, and where it takes place. Objectives for a year might read like this.

By the end of the year, children in the three-year-old class at First Church will have
— Heard stories about Jesus' birth, about how Jesus taught, and about his death and resurrection;
— Learned two or three songs of faith;
— Enjoyed being in Sunday school;
— Become familiar with their room in church;
— Participated in a mission project.

These objectives are fairly broad. They do, however, give a sense of direction for what will happen over a year's time. Yearly objectives start you on your journey. If in March you find you still have not had a mission project, you need to get busy and plan one. If you find yourself ahead of schedule, you can add to these goals throughout the year.

PLANNING FOR A QUARTER

After planning for the year, plan for each quarter. This planning is best done four times a year after you receive the quarterly material for the three months ahead. Even if you teach alone, find a friend or a teacher in another age level to plan with you. You will come up with more ideas by working together. The following guidelines may be helpful in your planning.

1. Read through all the material for the quarter. Read both the teacher's material and the students' material. Look through the class packet information and listen to the songs. As you do so, note ideas that appeal to you. Underline activities that you think will appeal to your class. Make notes in the margin of the teacher book, adding your own ideas.

2. Read through all the suggested Scripture for the quarter. Star those passages that you feel need more study. Talk with a friend about the meaning of the passages. Make notes in the margins of your teacher book and mark which stories and verses you want to emphasize most in your class.

3. Write your quarterly objectives. These might read as follows: By

the end of the fall quarter, children in the three-year-old class at First Church will

- Know the names of their teachers and of other children in their class at Sunday school;

- Be able to sing together "God Loves You";

- Be able to say together, "We love because God first loved us";

- Feel comfortable in their room at Sunday school;

- Experience ways the church cares for others.

4. Look at the equipment and supplies needed for each lesson. Are there items you should be collecting now for later in the quarter? It's hard to gather twelve egg cartons the Saturday night before Sunday's lesson. Make a master list of unusual equipment and supplies. Call the church office and ask for a list to be placed in the church bulletin or newsletter requesting items you may have a hard time collecting. If you buy your own supplies, mark on your calendar those items that will be needed each week. If someone else in the church buys supplies, make a list for that person with the date you need the supplies.

5. Consider your room arrangement. Do you want to make any changes for this quarter? Maybe you want to add a large cardboard box for the children to make into a church over the next few weeks. Maybe you want to add a reading corner with beanbag chairs and pillows on the floor. Now is the time to take down old pictures and bulletin boards and to put up material important for this quarter's study.

6. Think about visitors to invite for specific lessons during this quarter. On your calendar, mark whom you would like to have visiting your class. Maybe it's a new baby with her parents. It could be the church organist. Perhaps it's another Sunday school class. Issue the invitations well in advance, then make a note to yourself to call and remind those you've invited the week prior to their visit.

PLANNING FOR A SESSION

One of my pet peeves is to hear someone say, "I really don't have time to plan. Give me something I can look over on Saturday night and then be able to teach on Sunday morning." How cheap a price we put on the importance of passing on the Christian faith. Maybe we need to ask ourselves if we really need Sunday school classes when we're willing to spend so little time planning.

The best planning takes place bit by bit during the week. You might spend twenty minutes one day and thirty minutes the next. Good planning is always accompanied by Bible study and meditation. Good planning starts as soon as the class has ended for this week. The following steps can guide your planning:

1. Read the Scripture for this week's lesson. Think about what this passage means to you, and what it will mean to the children you teach. Read the background material provided in the teacher book and make use of commentaries for additional information. Write down what you think the main idea of the passage is.

2. Check the main idea and purposes listed for this lesson in your teacher book. Do these make sense to you in light of the Scripture you've just studied? Change and adapt the materials to fit your class.

3. List the activities you think best relate to the Scripture passage and to the purposes for the lesson.

4. Plan for the beginning of class time. What will help children enter into the room and into the lesson? Do you need to greet each child at the door? Do you need to make nametags?

5. Plan for the end of class time. What will help the children make a smooth transition from class to parents? Do you need to end with a group prayer, then keep the children together in a circle until their parents arrive? Is it better for your class to be involved in coloring or working on a project until their parents come?

6. Estimate the time for each category of activity. Do you have enough time to do all you plan to do? Will you need ten minutes for together time? Will the children spend twenty minutes in interest centers? Refer to Chapter 2 for suggested schedules.

7. List all the supplies you need for this lesson. Include even those that seem routine, such as crayons, paper, and so forth.

8. If you are teaching in a team, decide who will do which activity.

9. Make an outline of your plan to post in the room. Then if you need to, you can refer to the outline easily during the session.

10. Decide what needs to go home for parents to use at home. Make sure you have enough leaflets, cards, or newsletters to give to each child's parents. Write a reminder for parents and post it outside the classroom.

11. Pray daily for God's guidance as you teach and plan. Pray for the children in your class, remembering their individual needs.

12. After the children have left the classroom, take a few moments to evaluate. What went well? What activities need to be repeated? Where did you need more time? What do you know not to use again? Whom do you need to contact during the week?

As you teach, you will gain more confidence in planning. Things that took hours at first will eventually take only minutes. But the need for planning never ends. You might like to use the planning sheet on the next page. Duplicate this and use one each week to plan your lesson.

PLANNING SHEET FOR TEACHING YOUNG CHILDREN

Date _____ Unit Title _____

Lesson Title _____

Main Idea _____

Scripture _____

Lesson Purposes _____

_____

Write center activities in circles, along with equipment and supplies needed

(Family Living)   (Art:)   (Books and Puzzles:)

Together Time: Story _____ Verse _____

Activities: _____

Music: _____

_____

(Blocks:)   (Wonder and Worship:)   (Music:)

Class time will begin by _____

Class time will end by _____

How Do You Work Together?

When you became a preschool teacher, you entered into a partnership. You became partners with children to learn and grow with them. You became partners with others on your teaching team to share in responsibilities and tasks as well as in the joys of teaching. You became partners with parents, who hope you will love and care for their children each time they leave them with you. You became partners with others who use the same room to care for the room as well as for the children. You became partners with others who offer childcare, choir practice, midweek activities, and worship for the children you teach.

All of you are involved in a shared ministry with children and have common goals for those children: that they may grow in faith development and discipleship. Sometimes your common ministry is hard to remember when rooms are left messy, equipment is not put up, and there is no communication among all those involved in programs for young children. Strive to insure that all the programs your church provides for young children work together harmoniously for the good of all the children who enter the doors of your church.

SHARING SPACE

It's not unusual for the preschool rooms of the church to be used more than any others. This schedule is a typical week in many churches:

Sunday:
8:30 A.M. — Childcare during congregational worship
9:45 A.M. — Sunday school
10:50 A.M. — Extended care during congregational worship
5:00 P.M. — Childcare for youth workers
7:00 P.M. — Childcare during administrative meetings

Monday to Friday:
  7:00 A.M. to 6:00 P.M. — Daycare
Monday to Friday evenings:
  Childcare for meetings
Wednesdays:
  7:00 P.M. — Children's choir and activities

When several workers and several groups of children use the same space, it's normal for conflicts to occur. Every church that has shared space has to work hard to keep everyone as happy as possible with the maintenance and care of that space.

If you share a room with others, keep in mind that what is important is your common goal that all children who use the space will be happy, will learn and grow together, and will be safe while they are together. It's important to have common agreements about the care of your children's rooms.

If all adults who teach in a room can meet together once a quarter, you can work out differences together. With busy schedules, doing so can be difficult; but by working together you insure that the room will be kept up so that all children have a clean, safe, stimulating place to learn and play.

The decisions you make should always be written down, and every teacher or leader should have the latest copy of the rules you have jointly created. In outlining ways to care for a room, consider the following rules for all who use the space:

1. Adults in charge are responsible for leaving the room clean when they complete their time in the room. This responsibility includes cleaning tabletops, chairs, and cabinet tops with a damp sponge; placing all trash in the trash cans; and sweeping up paper scraps, glitter, and so forth.
2. After every use of the room return supplies and equipment to assigned storage places. This responsibility includes placing puzzle pieces back in puzzles, returning books to book racks, putting blocks back on shelves, and so forth.
3. Protect areas where messy activities occur. Put plastic on the floor where you have water play. Place newspaper on the floor underneath painting areas. Use play dough on tables, not on the floor.
4. Assign display area and storage space for each group using the space, and honor one another's displays.

CHAPTER 7

5. Turn out lights, leave no water running, and adjust room temperature when your time in the room is finished.

Often, problems with equipment and space arise from unsupervised groups of children playing with the toys in a room. When this happens, equipment gets broken, puzzle pieces are lost, and the room is often left in a mess. It can be a good idea to lock all classrooms when they are not scheduled for use.

WORKING WITH THE HOME

Teachers of preschoolers have more contact with parents than teachers of older children and youth do. The parents are more likely to bring their child to you, looking in on what you are doing and checking that the place they're leaving their child is good.

It is important to know what is happening at home. Young children express their emotions through their actions. If there has been a death in the home, if a new baby has arrived, if parents are going through divorce, often children will act out these hurts in the classroom. They may become clinging, wanting to be held all morning. They may hit and kick other children, retreating into their anger. They may become fearful.

Children react to the small events as well as the large events in their lives. They may be fussy because they are teething or are being toilet trained or are starting daycare. If you have no knowledge of the child's home life, you may label a child slow-to-learn, hyperactive, or uncooperative when the child is merely trying to cope with unsettling events.

You accumulate information about the home slowly and by building bridges of friendship with persons in the child's home. Here are a few ways to build these bridges:

1. Use the information sheets provided in *The First Three Years* (Discipleship Resources, 1995) or make your own information sheets on each child. Include the child's name, birthday, parents' names, names of others who live in the home, names of pets, weekday school the child attends, favorite foods, allergies, favorite activities, and fears. When you have a substitute, share this information with him or her before he or she teaches.
2. Visit the home of each child. Make an appointment first. The visit need not be lengthy.

3. Make phone calls and send home letters about activities you are doing in Sunday school.
4. Follow up on absences. If the child is with another parent every other week, make a note of these regular absences.
5. Celebrate birthdays in the class. Birthdays are important to children. Work with parents to prepare a snack or plan a time for singing to the birthday child.
6. Send home the weekly leaflets, showing parents suggested activities for follow-up during the week.
7. Post the day's lesson plan outside the classroom and ask parents to read what you will be doing.
8. Plan or suggest topics for parent classes, based on conversations you have with parents about needs related to discipline, sharing faith, using the Bible, getting children to listen, and so forth.
9. Type up a list of the children in your class, including addresses and parents' names and distribute these to all parents and to church staff.
10. Call on family members for help with special class projects such as field trips, class cleanup days, and parties.
11. Have an open house for parents one or two times a year so that children can share with parents what they've experienced in class.
12. Alert the pastor to family needs. You may be the first contact when a death occurs. You can provide crucial information for pastoral visits. Likewise, the pastor can provide you with information about the family that might be helpful.
13. If you teach infants or toddlers, work with your nursery home visitors. If your church does not have anyone who fills that role, lobby for such a position when you meet in your children's council or other administrative group. These visitors, who maintain home contact with parents during those childhood years when families find it most difficult to come regularly to church and to Sunday school, can be important advocates for parents and children.

What a privilege to touch the life of a child. And what a joy to receive from children the gifts of hugs, smiles, tears, laughter. As a partner in ministry, you guide the lives of the children you teach. Guard this gift well. Use the talents given to you by God. And grow in faith together.

A WORD FROM THE AUTHOR

I remember little about my own preschool years in Sunday school. I do remember going, and I remember the names of some of my teachers. I remember most, though, feeling thoroughly comfortable at church. We went often: twice on Sunday, on Wednesday nights, and at any other time there were special services. I felt at home when I was at church (and I still do).

I began to appreciate what had been done for me as a child when I became a graduate student at Scarritt College. For the first time, I began to reflect on the teaching I had received in the church. I began to try to remember my teachers and classmates and the experiences we shared.

When I entered Scarritt, I was committed to working with youth. I had taught youth in Sunday school, had been a youth counselor, had served as a youth director, and had never worked with anyone under twelve years of age. I knew youth—what they liked, how they learned, how to talk with them. I fully expected to continue working with youth through field assignments at Scarritt.

My adviser, Carrie Lou Goddard, changed those expectations. I was surprised, upset, and scared to find out I would be teaching three-year-olds at the Children's Center, our on-campus weekday preschool. I didn't know how three-year-olds acted, talked, learned, or played. I was sure that they did all these things differently from junior highs, but I knew little else about them.

To my delight I discovered that I had a talent for teaching young children, and I developed a love for doing so. Although relating to children came naturally to me, I still had a need to know what children are like, however. My story may or may not be like yours. Nevertheless, whatever talents you bring to the teaching of young children will be enhanced as you add knowledge about the ways children learn and develop.

My hope is that children everywhere can have adult friends and teachers who keep the needs of the child first in their minds. That thought has guided me in writing this book. For what I received as a child, I thank those who taught me at Central Avenue United Methodist Church, Batesville, Arkansas. They took my hand in theirs and started me on a lifelong journey of faith.

FOR FURTHER READING

ABOUT YOUNG CHILDREN

The First Three Years: A Guide for Ministry With Infants, Toddlers, and Two-Year-Olds, edited by Mary Alice Gran (Discipleship Resources, 1995)

How Do Our Children Grow, by Delia Touchton Halverson (Abingdon Press, 1993)

ABOUT PLANNING AND TEACHING

Foundations: Shaping the Ministry of Christian Education in Your Congregation (Discipleship Resources, 1993)

Planning for Christian Education: A Practical Guide for Your Congregation, edited by Carol F. Krau (Discipleship Resources, 1994)

Seven Ways of Learning, by Barbara Bruce (Abingdon Press, 1996)

Teaching Preschoolers in the Christian Community, by Phoebe Anderson (Pilgrim Press, 1994)

ABOUT TEACHING THE BIBLE

Adventures With the Bible: A Sourcebook for Teachers of Children, by Dorothy Jean Furnish (Abingdon Press, 1995)

The Bible in Christian Education, by Iris V. Cully (Augsburg, 1995)

Experiencing the Bible With Children, by Dorothy Jean Furnish (Abingdon Press, 1990).

RESOURCES FOR USE WITH YOUNG CHILDREN

Bible Zone: Where the Bible Comes to Life, Preschool FunAction Experience Kit, by Daphna Flegal (Abingdon Press, 1997)

Don't Just sit There: Bible Stories That Move You, for Ages 3–5, by Daphna Flegal (Abingdon Press, 1997)

New Invitation Toddlers and Twos, teacher book, quarterly class kits and quarterly sets of Bible Verse Picture Cards, edited by George Donigian and Barbara Snell (Abingdon Press, 1995)

Play! Think! Grow! 234 Activities for Christian Growth, edited by Doris Willis (Abingdon Press, 1992)